BLAST OFF!
THE SUN

CUSTOMER S

Helen and David Orme

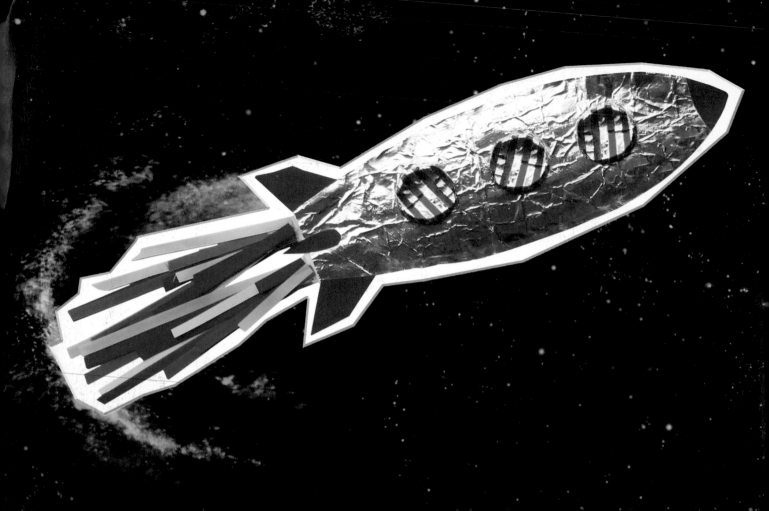

Copyright © ticktock Entertainment Ltd 2007
First published in Great Britain in 2007 by ticktock Media Ltd.,
Unit 2, Orchard Business Centre, North Farm Road,
Tunbridge Wells, Kent, TN2 3XF

ticktock project editor: Julia Adams
ticktock project designer: Emma Randall

We would like to thank: Sandra Voss, Tim Bones, James Powell,
Indexing Specialists (UK) Ltd.

ISBN 978 1 84696 048 2 pbk
ISBN 978 1 84696 550 0 hbk
Printed in China
A CIP catalogue record for this book is available from the British Library.

Picture credits
t=top, b=bottom, c=centre, l-left, r=right, bg=background
Art Directors: 20; Corbis: 21tr; NASA: 1all, 6bl, 7br, 8tl, 10, 11bl, 12br, 17bc, 22bl, 23 all; Science Photo Library: 4/5bg
(original), 5tr, 9tr, 9c, 18; Shutterstock: front cover, 2/3bg, 7bl, 13 all, 19 all, 22tr, 24bg; ticktock picture archive: 6/7bg, 7tl, 8br,
10/11, 11tr, 12tl, 14, 15 all, 16, 17tr, 21bl, 14/15bg, 18/19bg, 22/23bg;
Every effort has been made to trace the copyright holders, and we apologise in advance for any unintentional omissions.
We would be pleased to insert the appropriate acknowledgements in any subsequent edition of this publication.

Contents

The Sun in the Solar System

The Sun is the centre of our **solar system**. Without it, the solar system would not exist! All the planets, moons and **asteroids** in our solar system **orbit** around it.

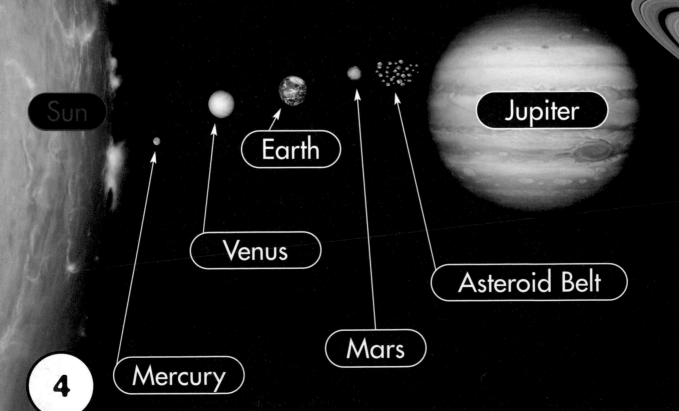

Sun

Mercury

Venus

Earth

Mars

Asteroid Belt

Jupiter

The Sun is a star. This means it creates light and heat. It is the closest star to Earth. You can see thousands of other stars in the sky. They are all much further away.

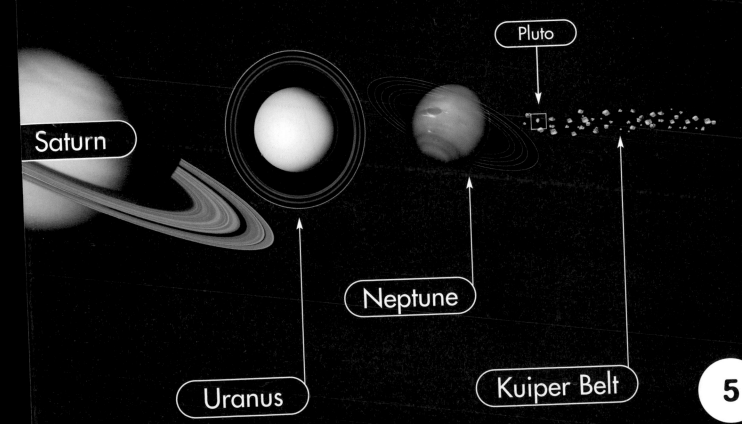

Pluto

Saturn

Uranus

Neptune

Kuiper Belt

Sun Facts

The Sun is the most important object in the **solar system**. It gives all the planets heat and light. Without the Sun, life would not be possible on Earth.

The centre of the Sun is mainly made of **hydrogen gas**. This gas turns into **helium gas**. When this happens, the Sun creates a lot of heat and light.

Centre: about 15 million °C

Sun

Corona: 5 million °C

Outer layer: 5,500 °C

The Sun is very, very hot. There is nothing we can compare the temperature with on Earth. We can't even imagine how hot the Sun is!

This picture shows how big the Sun is compared to the Earth. The Sun looks small from Earth because it is so far away.

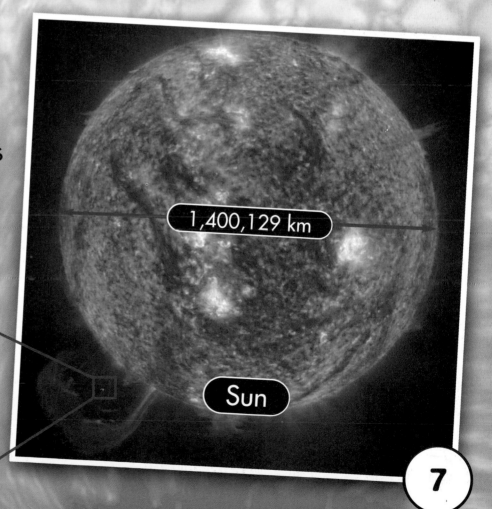

1,400,129 km

Sun

12,756 km

Earth

The Birth of the Sun

The Sun began its life billions of years ago. Before the Sun was there, our **solar system** did not exist!

Billions of years ago, a great cloud of gas and dust began to form.

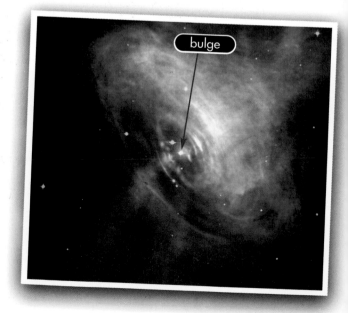

bulge

This cloud of gas began to form a spinning disk with a huge bulge in the middle. The disk began spinning faster and faster.

The huge bulge kept heating up until it started turning **hydrogen gas** into **helium gas**.

The great bulge was turning into the Sun. At the same time, the planets were formed from the rest of the gassy disk.

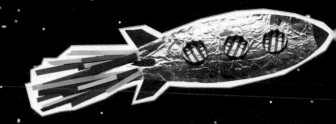

The Sun's Life

The Sun is about 4½ billion years old! Like people, animals and planets, it was born, will have a lifetime, and then it will die.

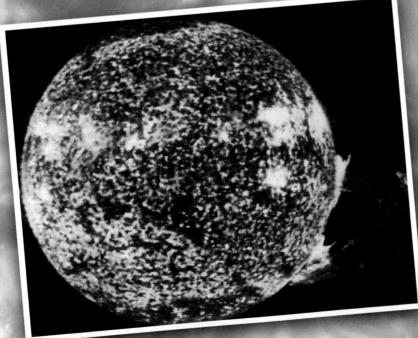

The Sun is made of **hydrogen gas**. The hydrogen gas is turning into **helium gas**. This creates a lot of heat.

Almost half of the hydrogen the Sun is made of has now turned into helium. It will take about 5 billion years for all the hydrogen to be used up.

When all the hydrogen has been turned into helium, the Sun will start to grow bigger. It will grow up to 100 times its original size! Then it will be called a Red Giant.

Sun

Red Giant

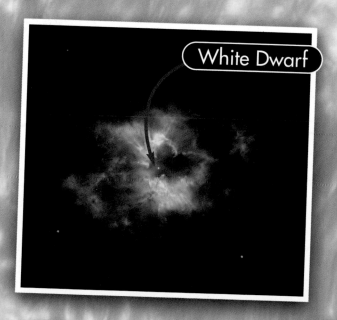

White Dwarf

Then the Sun's outer layers will start turning into a cloud of gas. The gas will slowly disappear and leave he Sun's centre. The Sun will start to cool down, although this will take millions of years. Stars like this are called White Dwarfs.

Sunspots and Flares

The Sun sometimes has spots on its outer layer. These are places where the temperature is lower.

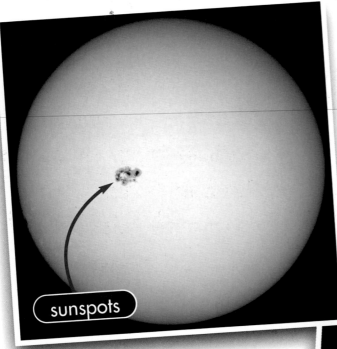

sunspots

Sunspots are not always in the same place on the Sun. Scientists have found out that every 11 years, the Sun has more sunspots than usual.

flare

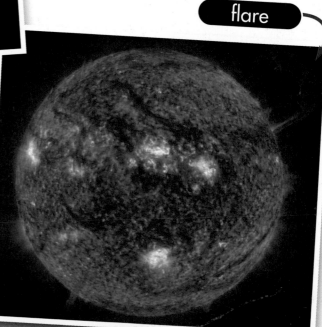

Sometimes there are huge explosions on the Sun. This means that extremely hot **particles** of the Sun are hurled into space. They are called flares.

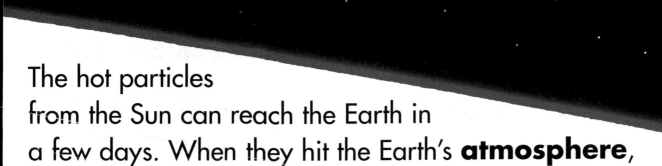

The hot particles
from the Sun can reach the Earth in
a few days. When they hit the Earth's **atmosphere**,
the sky lights up in different colours.

This photograph shows
what happens when hot
particles from the Sun reach
the Earth's atmosphere in
the north. This is called
Aurora Borealis, or
Northern Lights.

Earth

This is a photograph
of the Aurora Australis,
or Southern Lights. You can
see them when the Sun's hot
particles reach the Earth's
atmosphere in the south.

Earth

Eclipses

Sometimes our Moon
moves between the Earth and the Sun.
When this happens all or part of the Sun
is covered over. This is called an eclipse.

Moon

This picture shows what happens when the
Moon moves between the Sun and the Earth.
The shadow marks the spot on Earth where you can
see the Moon blocking out the Sun entirely.
This is called a total eclipse.

Moon covering
part of the Sun

This is a **partial** eclipse of the Sun. It means that only a part of the Sun is covered by the Moon.

Sun

Moon covering
the Sun

This is a total eclipse of the Sun. It doesn't happen very often. When it happens, it is possible to see the glowing gas (corona) that is around the Sun.

glowing
Corona

Winds and Rays

The Sun doesn't just create heat and light. All sorts of **rays** come from the Sun. Some of them are dangerous to all life on Earth.

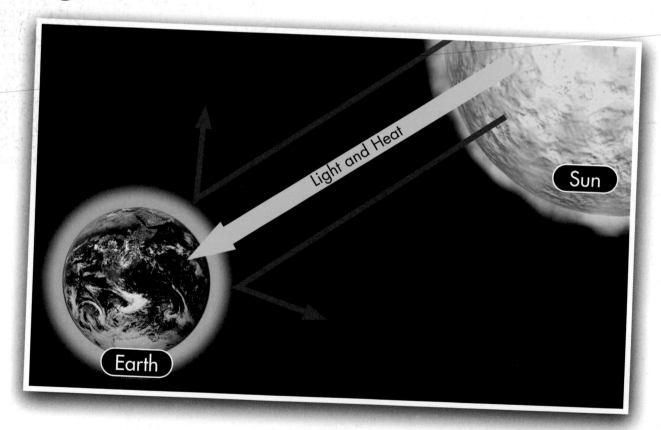

Light and Heat

Sun

Earth

This picture shows the heat and the light from the Sun reaching Earth. The red arrows show the dangerous rays. The **atmosphere** helps to stop dangerous rays coming through to Earth.

The
on
hum
cou
sun
anii
plan
fruit

Particles pour out of the Sun at high speed. This is called the solar wind. It travels at over one million kilometres an hour!

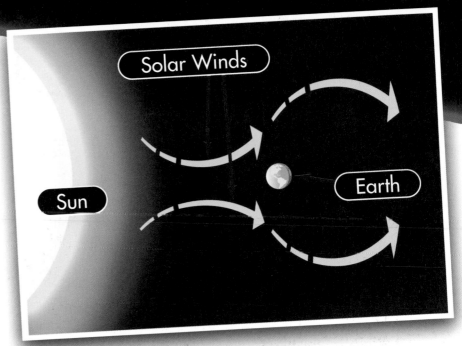

Solar Winds

Sun

Earth

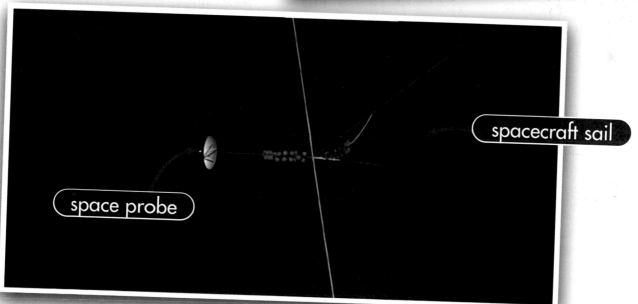

spacecraft sail

space probe

Some scientists think the solar wind could be used to push spacecraft along, like sailing ships!

Glossary

Asteroids Rocky objects that orbit the Sun. Most asteroids orbit the Sun between Mars and Jupiter.

Astronomers People who study space, often using telescopes.

Atmosphere The gases that surround a star, planet or moon.

Chariot A cart that is drawn by horses.

Helium gas A gas that is lighter than air. We use helium to fill balloons!

Hydrogen gas A very light gas. It is extremely explosive.

NASA (short for National Aeronautics and Space Administration) An American group of scientists and astronauts who research space.

Orbit The path planets or other objects take around the Sun, or satellites take around planets.

Partial When something is not complete.

Particles Tiny amounts or very small pieces of something.

Rays Beams of light and warmth. Some rays are dangerous because they are very harmful to life on Earth.

Satellites Moons or man-made objects that are in orbit round a planet.

Solar system The Sun and everything that is in orbit around it.

Space probe A spacecraft sent from Earth to explore the solar system. It can collect samples and take pictures.

Index